PRAISE FOR THE FIRST EDITION

"A great book fo̶̶̶̶̶̶̶̶ ̶̶̶̶̶̶̶̶ Christmas
story, and ̶̶̶̶̶̶̶̶ ̶̶̶̶̶̶̶̶ It's both
creative an̶̶̶̶ ̶̶̶̶̶̶̶̶ esh and
faithful. I h̶̶̶̶

KEVIN ̶̶̶̶̶̶̶̶ ̶̶̶̶, *Crazy Busy*; Senior Pastor,
Ch̶̶̶̶ ̶̶̶̶ant Church, Matthews, Charlotte, NC

"A humorous, piercing and, above all, truthful book that challenges our preconceptions of Christmas. Carl writes with wit and a real grasp of modern minds to show us that Jesus can't stay in the manger."

RICO TICE, Founder, Christianity Explored Ministries;
Author, *A Very Different Christmas*

"A great book for introducing people to the real and wonderful Jesus of history—lots of myth-busting, truth and humour."

LIZZY SMALLWOOD, Speaker and Author

"An accessible, faithful guide to the actual Christmas story. Let this book help you get to grips with the reality and purpose of Christmas, and introduce you to the person who is at the center of it all."

TREVIN WAX, Vice President, NAMB;
Author, *Rethink Your Self*

"This book blows the dust off the first Christmas story! It's fast paced and witty, and will help anyone discover what really happened when Jesus was born."

LEE MCMUNN, Author, Identity Course; Senior Minister,
Trinity Church Scarborough, North Yorkshire

CHRISTMAS

UNCUT

Christmas Uncut (2nd edition)
© The Good Book Company, 2023.

Published by
The Good Book Company

thegoodbook.com | thegoodbook.co.uk
thegoodbook.com.au | thegoodbook.co.nz | thegoodbook.co.in

Unless indicated, all Scripture references are taken from the Holy Bible,
New International Version. Copyright © 2011 Biblica, Inc. Used by
permission.

All rights reserved. Except as may be permitted by the Copyright Act,
no part of this publication may be reproduced in any form or by any
means without prior permission from the publisher.

Carl Laferton has asserted his right under the Copyright, Designs and
Patents Act 1988 to be identified as author of this work.

Cover design by Drew McCall

ISBN: 9781784989156 | JOB-007197 | Printed in India

CONTENTS

INTRODUCTION

What did you most want the December you were six? I wanted to be one of the three kings in my school nativity play. And I particularly wanted to be the king who got to wear the gold cloak. (It was actually an old curtain, but it looked good.)

The only problem was my teacher, Mrs Abblett. She decided to give out the roles based on acting ability. Since my approach to speaking on stage was "say it as loud as possible, as fast as possible", this meant the end of my kingly dream. Instead, I got the not-so-glamorous role of the rear end of Donkey Number Two. (Thankfully, it was a non-speaking part.)

And, as every six-year-old knows, there's only one donkey in the nativity story. Nowhere does it say that as Mary set out for Bethlehem on her steed, she took a spare along in case of breakdown. Or that Donkey Number One had a friend who was at a loose end that day and came along for the ride.

I was devastated. Not only was I not a main part—I wasn't even a bit-part. I was a no-part. Or, to be more accurate, the rear end of a no-part.

NO DONKEYS AT ALL

But in fact, I needn't have been so disappointed. Yes, there wasn't a Donkey Number Two at the first Christmas. But here's the thing I discovered years later: there wasn't even a Donkey Number One. The original, real-life Mary didn't ride a donkey. And there weren't any kings, either.

The donkey and the kings are famous parts of the nativity story. But they're nowhere to be seen in the real Christmas history.

When children act out the nativity, often it actually doesn't have that much in common with the historical Christmas. Over time, we've cut huge, crucial bits out. We've added nice but completely made-up details. We've made it into a tale for children and forgotten the real events.

We've turned Christmas history into a nativity play.

I don't want to be a spoilsport. I've enjoyed watching my own kids play a shepherd, an angel, a sheep, and an alien (yes, really)—though never, sadly, a king. Nativity plays are part of the whole Christmas experience, along with desperate last-minute shopping and sending cards to people who you didn't make the effort to see last year and won't make the effort to see next year either. It's just that the real Christmas is much more interesting than what we've turned it into. It's worth rescuing and retelling.

So let's begin. At the first Christmas, Mary wasn't waving to her parents in the front row. The angels weren't wearing last year's tinsel stuck onto old white sheets. Joseph's dad wasn't annoying a shepherd's grandma by standing up in front of her to record his son's big moment.

What there was at the first Christmas was scandal. Controversy. Massacres. Mystery.

MORE THAN HISTORY

The real Christmas is a great story. But it's more than that. This isn't simply a 2,000-year-old history; it's a story that speaks to us today—about our life, our world, our future. What happened way back then is still changing and shaping millions of people's lives in the 21st century. What really happened at Christmas still really matters today, to all of us.

That's the Christmas story this book is about. Each chapter, or scene, is in two parts. First, *What really happened* to real people. In each of these sections, you'll see some words in this **kind of text**. These are words taken straight out of the Bible* and are the really

---

* I use sentences from the Bible to show what really happened in human history. If you want to know why, you might like to flick to "Yes, but... isn't a lot of this made up?" at the end of the book on page 69. And if you'd like to read about the historical Christmas in the Bible, you can find it in Matthew 1 v 18 – 2 v 23 (that is, chapter 1, verse 18 through to chapter 2, verse 23); and in Luke 1 v 26 – 2 v 40.

important ones. Those in normal text are written by me, just to help you grasp what was going on.

And second, in *Why it really matters* we'll see why what happened way back then still has significance for how we live today. In each scene, this part will focus on one character from the Christmas history.

This is not a cute nativity play (though we'll mention incidents from various nativity plays as we go). It's not fluffy, childish or dull. There are some parts you probably wouldn't want a young child even to know about.

It's the real Christmas—uncut.

SHOCK AND SCANDAL

Mary

It's the height of ambition for most 5-year-old girls—and often for their mothers, too. But in every school, church or kindergarten, only one girl each year can reach the dizzying height of playing Mary in the nativity play.

A few years back, one of my god-daughters was selected. She only had one line—which she forgot—and one job, holding the baby Jesus—which she did. Around the neck.

But those were minor details. She was Mary. Proud girl. Proud parents. All good.

Yet, in a way, it's strange that parents want their daughters to be Mary. We're essentially dreaming that our child will play a teenage mother who got herself pregnant in a very suspicious way and whose life nearly fell apart because of it. Because that's what happened to the real Mary.

WHAT REALLY HAPPENED

To begin with, it was just a normal day; by the end, her life would have changed for ever.

But this story doesn't start with a teenage girl in northern Israel. It starts with God. It starts in heaven.

God sent the angel Gabriel to Nazareth, a town in Galilee, to a virgin pledged to be married to a man named Joseph.*

The virgin's name was Mary.

The angel went to her and said, "Greetings, you who are highly favoured! The Lord is with you."

Unsurprisingly, **Mary was greatly troubled at his words and wondered what kind of greeting this might be**. She knew from the history of her people, the Jews, how rare it was for one of God's messengers to visit them, and that when an angel did appear, it usually meant that things were about to get shaken up. And here she was in the middle of it all.

But the angel said to her, "Do not be afraid, Mary, you have found favour with God. You will conceive and give birth to a son, and you are to call him Jesus.

"He will be great and will be called the Son of the Most High. The Lord God will give him the throne of

---

* Words straight from the Bible are **in bold like this**.

his father David"—the David who had ruled over Israel a thousand years earlier, and was still remembered and loved as the Jews' greatest-ever king.

"His kingdom will never end."

Mary was in shock, but she was still able to think clearly. She was about to be pregnant—and yet she knew that was impossible.

"How will this be," Mary asked the angel, "since I am a virgin?"

The angel answered, "The Holy Spirit—God himself—will come on you, and the power of the Most High will overshadow you. So the holy one to be born will be called the Son of God. For no word from God will ever fail. He can make it happen."

Mary didn't fully grasp what was happening; but she knew that, for some reason, she'd just been brought into one of God's plans.

"I am the Lord's servant," Mary answered. "May your word to me be fulfilled."

Then the angel left her.

Explaining to Joseph what had happened wasn't easy. The two of them were engaged, but they hadn't slept together (they were waiting until they were married); now she was pregnant. Joseph wasn't convinced by Mary's "God is the father" explanation; but he was a kind man, and did not want to expose her to the public disgrace that would come her way if people found out that she'd slept with another guy. So he had in mind to break off their engagement **quietly**.

But after he had considered this, an angel of the Lord appeared to him in a dream and said, "Joseph, do not be afraid to take Mary home as your wife, because what is conceived in her is from the Holy Spirit.

"She will give birth to a son, and you are to give him the name Jesus."

Joseph knew the promises God had made to his people through the centuries. He knew God had promised that a child would be born who would, in some amazing way, be God himself. He knew God had said that this child would be born to a virgin. And that virgin had turned out to be his wife-to-be! Mary didn't deserve him leaving her; and she desperately needed him to love her.

When Joseph woke up, he did what the angel had commanded him and took Mary home as his wife. But he didn't sleep with her **until she gave birth**.

Read the full story: Luke 1 v 26-38; Matthew 1 v 18-25

WHY IT REALLY MATTERS

A nativity play begins with smiles and carols. The real Christmas began with scandal, shame and shock.

SCANDAL

Here's the scandal. Mary was a normal girl living in a nothing town called Nazareth, in the north of Israel.

She was probably 14 or 15—and (as was normal in that society) engaged to be married. But, before Joseph had touched her, she fell pregnant.

Today, that might prompt a bit of gossip—nothing more. Then, it was hugely scandalous. They took marriage seriously in Israel—so seriously that adultery could get you stoned to death. And that included anyone who was engaged—like Mary.

So that's what Mary faced. Not just dirty looks and cutting comments from other women, but a lifetime of struggle and loneliness, and the real possibility of death. But they don't mention those things in nativity plays.

SHAME

Here's the shame. Imagine being Joseph. There aren't many things more humiliating than being cheated on, and that's what the neighbours would assume Mary had done. It's amazing that Joseph was prepared to break their engagement off quietly, rather than letting everyone know what Mary did. It's even more amazing that he ended up sticking by her.

They don't mention those things in nativity plays, either.

SHOCK

And here's the shock. *All this was God's doing.*

I don't know how you imagine God, if you do at all. Maybe some old guy sitting up in the sky? Maybe some amazingly powerful force who, quite frankly, has more interesting things to do than care about our little lives? Maybe some distant being who really has no idea what life is actually like here on Planet Earth?

But here's the God of the Bible. He's a God who gets involved. Who turns lives upside down. Who doesn't act as we might expect.

He's a God who came and lived on earth, as a human.

That's the big shock. Not that a teenage girl got pregnant and the father wasn't the man she was engaged to. Not that a guy decided to stick by his fiancé, even though he wasn't the father.

No—the shock is that the baby "will be called the Son of God".

WHO IS GOD?

This baby was God coming to live in human history. This baby would be human (Mary was his mother); but he would also be God. He was God's Son, who had existed with God the Father (who we normally just call God) and God the Holy Spirit since before the creation of the world.

And so here's a glimpse of who God is. He's Father, Son and Spirit. He's existed as this three-in-one God, in perfect love and relationship within himself, for eternity.

That sounds quite strange. And it is! But it's also exciting. Because if this God is all about love and rela-tionships, then the universe he's made will be about love and relationships too. It's not about power, about the survival of the fittest and scrabbling to reach the top. It's not about possessions, about getting the most you can and always striving for more. It's not about pointlessness, about you being a random collection of atoms that gather for a while as you, until they start to disperse at the point that we call death. No, the God of love and relationship has made you to enjoy a life of love which lasts and relationships that work, just as he does within himself. This makes sense of our impulse to love, our feelings of loneliness, and our desire to feel that there's a point to life. Of course we feel these things—we were created by a God who is all about love, and who created us to enjoy that kind of life.

That's a God worth knowing. And that's the God who was going to be born to Mary: God the Son, coming to live on earth.

MIND-BLOWING

I don't know about you, but I struggle to get my head around that. The God of eternity, who knows and controls everything, becoming a baby who needs changing, feeding, burping. My mind can't work that out!

But then, there are lots of things that overload my brain—like the fact that light can travel from the sun to here in 8.3 minutes. That's a speed, according to Google, of 186,000 miles or 300,000 km per second. My mind can't really understand how something can travel so fast. (Science was never my strongest subject at school.) But despite that, I accept that light does indeed travel at that speed.

We'll never understand how God could travel so far—from his throne in heaven to the womb of a woman in Israel. But he did. The angel said that this baby "will be called the Son of God". God came to earth, as one of us, to live in the world he'd created.

So what would God as a human be like? What did he want to tell us? What was he coming to do?

At this point in her story, Mary had only a vague idea. But the night her son was born, things would start to become clearer.

MEETING ROYALTY

The Angel

From the moment when the couple in charge of that year's nativity decided that the children involved would improvise their own words, there was always a serious chance things would go wrong.

The performance began smoothly enough. The children were loving it—their parents (and grandparents, and aunts, and neighbours) were too.

But then the angels appeared to the shepherds.

The tea-towel-head-dress-wearing young shepherds had been told that angels were not cuddly or cute—that they were, in fact, scary. And one of the shepherds had thought hard about how he would react if he saw a terrifying angel. As the blonde-haired girl playing "chief angel", complete with white sheet and gold tinsel, appeared on stage and opened her mouth to begin speaking, he jumped up.

"ARGHHHHHHH!" he shouted. "Run!" And with that, the shepherds disappeared off the stage, leaving several toy lambs and a deserted chief angel. She announced the birth of Jesus to an empty stage.

WHAT REALLY HAPPENED

Mary's pregnancy went without a hitch; her birth plan, however, was severely disrupted.

When the Roman emperor **Augustus issued a decree that a census should be taken of the entire Roman world**, he didn't know, and wouldn't have cared, that Mary was nine months pregnant. All his subjects had to go **to their own town to register**; and so Mary and Joseph faced an 80-mile trip **from the town of Nazareth in Galilee to Judea, to Bethlehem the town of David, because** Joseph **belonged to the house and line of David**, who'd been king a thousand years before.

While they were there, the time came for the baby to be born, and Mary **gave birth to her firstborn, a son. She wrapped him in cloths and placed him in** an animal food trough, **because there was no guest room available for them**.

It wasn't exactly the easiest time and place to give birth. But Mary wasn't the only person awake that night. **There were shepherds living out in the fields near by, keeping watch over their flocks at night**. They too were far from home; they too had no bed.

Being a shepherd was a dirty, boring, lonely job.

Someone had to do it—and everyone else was glad it wasn't them. But it was to these shepherds that God the Father chose to announce the arrival of his Son.

An angel of the Lord appeared to them, and the glory of the Lord shone around them.

They were terrified. They knew that coming face to face with God's glory—his pure, unmasked perfection—was too much for mere people.

But the angel said to them, "Do not be afraid. I bring you good news that will cause great joy for all the people. Today in the town of David a Saviour has been born to you; he is the Messiah, the Lord. This will be a sign to you that what I'm saying is true: **you will find a baby wrapped in cloths and lying in a manger."**

The shepherds began to pick themselves off the floor. They had seen God's glory and lived. The heavenly messengers appeared to have brought good news about a baby, not bad news about their inability to live in God's presence.

Suddenly a great company of angels appeared, **praising God**.

And then, as quickly as they'd appeared, the shepherds realised **the angels had left them and gone into heaven**. Darkness returned; and all that was left was a flock of startled sheep and a few stunned shepherds.

Read the full story: Luke 2 v 1-14

WHY IT REALLY MATTERS

I'D LIKE YOU TO MEET...

How do you introduce people?

You're at a family gathering with a new boyfriend or girlfriend, or you're at a meeting with a new colleague. How do you introduce them to everyone else?

It seems to me that we usually do it by saying who they're related to or what it is they do. It's "John, this is Lizzie, my girlfriend" or "Lizzie, this is John, my grandma's nephew". Or it's "Hannah, this is Tom, who's joined us in the marketing team" or "Tom, this is Hannah, our regional manager".

Family relationships and job descriptions tell you a lot about someone. And, through an angel on a hillside, God introduced his Son to the world in exactly the same way: by outlining who he was related to and what his job was.

DOUBLE ROYALTY

So, who was this hours-old baby related to? "Today in the town of David," the angel said, a baby had been born who was "the Lord".

The angel was pointing to the baby's two family trees. On one side, he was related to King David—Israel's greatest-ever ruler, who was still remembered and respected (a little like how Winston Churchill or America's founding fathers are still remembered and respected by many today for their achievements—

though with less debate about his legacy!). That's why Mary had to give birth on the floor of an animal shelter instead of the bed in her house. Both she and Joseph were part of David's family, which came from Bethlehem; so they'd had to travel there for the census.

David's family had fallen a long way. Joseph didn't sit on a throne in the capital, Jerusalem; he made wooden chairs in Nazareth, a rural backwater. But God had promised that one day David's line would get their throne back. And Jesus was descended from David.

The other family tree was the one Gabriel had already told Mary about. "The Lord" was a title used for God. And when a heavenly angel uses this title in the midst of a cloud of God's glory, the implication is pretty clear: this baby is divine.

God introduces Jesus as human royalty and as heavenly royalty.

ENTER THE KING

So what job had this royal baby come to do?

> *"Today in the town of David a Saviour has been born to you; he is the Messiah, the Lord."*

God had given his Son two jobs. First, he was (still is, in fact) *Messiah*.

Those shepherds probably hadn't spent much time in the town's school or the local Jewish synagogue. But they would have known just how significant the arrival of God's Messiah was. Messiah—or, in the Greek that the elites spoke in those days, "Christ"—was a title which meant "God's promised King".

For centuries, God had been promising to send his King into the world. Not just any king, but *the* King. The King who would rule perfectly. The King who would rule selflessly. The King who would rule for ever.

The King whose rule would guarantee security for life and bring satisfaction to life.

The King who would rule not only Israel, as David had, but the whole world. The King who would restore the world to how God intended, to be the perfect place he'd created. All of that was summed up in the word "Messiah".

Over the centuries, God had given clues so that people would be able to recognise the Messiah when he finally appeared. He'd spoken through his messengers (prophets) and told his people that the Messiah would be one of David's descendants. He'd told them that the Messiah would be born in Bethlehem.

And now, on a hillside outside Bethlehem, he announced that, at last, the Messiah had been born.

THE END OF DISAPPOINTMENT

Who your leader is really matters.

The day after the US election in 2016, I was on a plane from London to Boston. No American on that plane that day thought that the leader their nation had chosen was irrelevant to their lives, their hopes, their safety and their futures. Some of them were feeling really pleased that Donald Trump was about to become the 45th president; some of them were (at quite some volume) feeling very much the opposite. Fast-forward to 2020, and Trump was out and Biden was in; and I imagine the scene on the plane that day would've been similar—some passengers delighted and others gutted.

Leadership matters. It's why we get annoyed with our leaders. It's why we feel let down by our leaders. It's why we get excited about possible future leaders.

And the problem is that sooner or later (and probably sooner) our leaders disappoint us. Either because of changes in circumstances or their own shortcomings, they don't keep their promises. They make mistakes. Of course they do. They're only human, and the mixture of power and pressure that goes with leadership tends to widen the cracks in our characters. We know we need good leaders; but finding them seems hard.

If only we could find someone good enough at ruling our country to give us, and everyone else, the security and satisfaction we want: someone who was always able to know what the right thing to do was and then was always unselfish enough to do it.

Some of us are still looking for a leader like that. Some of us have given up, deciding none of them will be good enough. Actually we're both right! Leadership *can* sort everything out; but no leader we can find is the leader who *will* sort it out.

The people who lived in 1st-century Israel were much the same. They'd put their hopes in judges, kings, warriors, homegrown rulers and foreign emperors; none of them had delivered. They'd learned to be as cynical about leaders' promises as most of us are.

They still wanted a ruler; it was just that they had learned through experience that only a perfect man could be a perfect ruler. And they hadn't found one.

Until now. Until God's angel said to some very ordinary people, *He's here*. The Messiah, God's promised King, who could actually deliver on his promises, had arrived.

That was great news for those shepherds then, and it's great news for us today. There is a ruler who offers to rule us perfectly, selflessly, for ever, giving us security throughout life and satisfaction in life. There's a ruler who can get rid of the things which stop our lives being as we'd like them to be: who can get rid of suffering, injustice, fear, even death.

There is a King who can establish endless perfection on earth. He's God's Messiah, and he's the leader we're all looking for.

A STRANGE ADDITION

But that's not all. This baby had a second job. The angel didn't only say the Messiah had been born—he also said that a "Saviour" had been born. Jesus' job wasn't only to be a ruler but also to be a rescuer.

Why did the people need rescuing? The answer to that question would be yet another shock; but the shepherds, and everyone else, would have to wait to find it out. For now, they were starting to come to terms with what had just happened out on their hillside...

TAKE A LOOK

The Shepherds

The nativity play was going well. Jesus had been born, the angels had announced his birth without too much waving (and no one had run away), and now Mary and Joseph were waiting for a visit from the shepherds.

It never happened.

From the side of the stage came raised voices. Instead of walking on, the shepherds had started to argue. "I'm meant to go on first!" "No, Mrs Cole said it was my turn." Before anyone could intervene, the shepherds were using their crooks to smack each other on the head.

Soon the three of them were in a full-on fight. Finally, a grown-up reached the battle, disentangled them, and pushed them through a door out of the hall.

The nativity play carried on. But that year, no shepherds visited the baby.

WHAT REALLY HAPPENED

The shepherds said to one another, "Let's go to Bethlehem and see this thing that has happened, which the Lord has told us about."

So they hurried off and found Mary and Joseph, and the baby, who was lying in the manger. It was just as they had been told.

When they had seen him, they spread the word concerning what had been told them about this child. Of course, everyone **who heard it** was **amazed at what the shepherds said to them**.

The shepherds themselves **returned** to their sheep and their fields and the darkness. Those things were just the same as they'd been several hours before; but life wasn't.

God could have chosen a royal palace to announce Jesus' birth, or a religious temple. He hadn't; he'd picked their field! They spent the rest of the night **glorifying and praising God for all the things they had heard and seen**.

Mary was simply exhausted. She knew the events of the past 24 hours were of life-changing, world-shaping significance. She also knew it would take a long time— perhaps her whole life—to process what had gone on. She **treasured up all these things and pondered them in her heart**.

Read the full story: Luke 2 v 15-20

WHY IT REALLY MATTERS

If God's Messiah, God's Son, really came to live in this world, that's of huge significance. It means that we can know what God is like. It means that we can know what God thinks of us. And it means that we can know how God designed us to live, and therefore what will make us happiest.

If God's Messiah was born and laid in a manger in Bethlehem, that's huge—for all people, in every place and in every time.

So the vital question facing the shepherds was: Was it true? Had the angel made it up? Had they made the angel up?! Was it all a dream, a mistake, a joke?

There was only one way to find out for sure. Sensibly, they said to each other, "Let's go to Bethlehem and see". The angel had told them they'd find a baby wrapped in cloths (this was normal enough) and lying in a manger—a food trough for animals (this was less normal).

The shepherds could go and look for themselves. Either this baby in a manger would be there, or he wouldn't. Either Jesus the Messiah had been born, or he hadn't. It was a question of fact.

FACT — OR FALSE

This is one of the great things about Christianity. It centres on claims about historical fact. You might think those claims are all true; or you might be very doubtful. But in the end, Christianity is not about feelings, or following the views of the family or culture you grew up in, or finding some secret knowledge; it's about facts of history. It's about whether or not this happened.

Either the Messiah was born and put in that manger on that night in that town, as angels announced his arrival—in which case, he's God's promised perfect King; or he wasn't, and they didn't, and Jesus is either a figment of someone's imagination or just a normal baby among thousands of normal babies born that year—in which case, Christianity's false, made up, and not worth your time.

CHECK — DON'T ASSUME

When the shepherds looked into it, they discovered it was all "just as they had been told". What they found in Bethlehem backed up the angel's claims on the hillside. It had happened. They checked it out, and found it was fact.

In the 21st century, many people just assume that Christianity is false. They don't check; they assume. Equally, some people just assume that the whole Jesus-the-Messiah thing is true, without thinking about it; and often, when their views are challenged, their faith falls over.

When I trained as a journalist, the man who taught us had been a sub-editor for years. He was a small Welsh guy, and he had two favourite lines, which I can still hear him saying as I write this.

One was, "That's useless (actually, he used a stronger, shorter word). Bin it!"

The other was, "Assume makes a donkey (again, he used a stronger, shorter word) out of u and me."

Time and again, he told us that when it comes to reporting, opinions and claims don't matter. What people think is irrelevant. What counts are facts. Don't assume you know the truth, he insisted. Check out the facts: what really happened?

That's what the shepherds did. And they found the angel's claim was true.

Unfortunately, we're 2,000 years too late to go and see the manger for ourselves. But we can still make sure we don't just assume one way or the other. Is this story facts or false? We can see whether Luke, the writer who tells us about the shepherds, was writing historical facts. We can see whether his story matches what else we know about that part of history. We can read the rest of his biography of Jesus and see if it has the ring of truth to it.

We can look into whether what happened at the beginning of Jesus' life is fact. And we can explore whether what happened at the end—when he died and then rose again—is really fact too.

I know people who, when they've begun to look into the Gospels' claims about Jesus, have been surprised by what they've found. I know that I was surprised too, when I began to look into them.

If you want to follow the shepherds and check out if the claims of Christianity are true, the best place to start is by grabbing a copy of Luke's biography, or "Gospel", about Jesus. And if you're wondering whether Luke's Gospel is genuinely historically reliable, page 69 will get you started and point you to some other things to read which go into more detail.

But for now, we need to leave the shepherds in their fields. Because the story's focus switches to a mysterious country hundreds of miles from the manger and the baby.

SCENE FOUR

WISE OR CRAZY?

The Magi

The first wise man, a seven-year-old boy, was really chuffed to be wearing a crown on stage, with everyone looking at him. He said his line and knelt down next to the manger to offer his gift to Jesus.

Then there was a pause.

He looked at the box in his hands, wrapped in beautiful, shiny gold paper. He began to look doubtful and to shuffle away from the manger.

"Give the baby Jesus your present," hissed the organiser from the edge of the stage, where she was trying to convince an angel not to pull her wings off her costume.

The wise man shook his head.

"Give Jesus your gift," said the organiser, striding onto the stage with a fixed smile and attempting to prise the boy's fingers off the present.

"No," squealed the wise man. "It's my gold box, and I'm keeping it."

WHAT REALLY HAPPENED

Although the Romans were in overall charge, they let a local guy rule Israel as king, to keep the peace and keep the taxes coming in. When Jesus was born, it was **during the time of King Herod**.

Some time after the shepherds visited the manger in Bethlehem, some **Magi**, or wise men, **from the east came to Jerusalem and asked, "Where is the one who has been born king of the Jews? We saw his star when it rose and have come to worship him."**

This was sensible. If the king of the Jews had come along, it made sense to look in the Jewish capital. But nobody knew what the Magi were talking about—Herod was king, same as always. And the star they had followed from their own country seemed to have disappeared from the sky. They kept asking around—and eventually news of these strange foreigners looking for a newborn king reached the royal palace.

When King Herod heard this he was disturbed, and all Jerusalem with him. When he had called together all people's chief priests and teachers of the law, he asked them where the Messiah was to be born.

This was an easy question for the religious leaders. They knew their Scriptures back to front. They knew what God had promised about the Messiah long ago through his messengers (called prophets). And they knew what God had told one of those prophets, Micah, seven hundred years earlier.

"In Bethlehem in Judea," they replied, "for this is what the prophet has written:

"'But you, Bethlehem, in the land of Judah, are by no means least among the rulers of Judah; for out of you will come a ruler who will shepherd my people Israel.'"

Then Herod called the Magi secretly and found out from them the exact time the star had appeared. He was guessing the wise men had spotted the star when the baby was born; and he wanted to know how old this so-called "king" was by now.

He sent them to Bethlehem and said, "Go and search carefully for the child. As soon as you find him, report to me, so that I too may go and worship him."

After they had heard the king, they went on their way, and the star they had seen when it rose went ahead of them until it stopped over the place where the child was. When they saw the star, they were overjoyed. On coming to the house, they saw the child with his mother Mary, and they bowed down and worshipped him.

Then they opened their treasures and presented him with gifts of gold, frankincense and myrrh. They had found the one they'd travelled so far to see.

Read the full story: Matthew 2 v 1-11

WHY IT REALLY MATTERS

BABY VISITORS

Do you know who visited you after you were born? According to my mum (I've heard this story several times now), I was visited by my dad, my grandparents, a couple of nurses, a doctor and Linda, a lady who was in hospital having a baby too.

In other words, my birth was so significant that I was visited by people who were either members of my family or in the hospital anyway.

But, as far as I'm aware, Queen Elizabeth II was not even informed that Carl Laferton had just entered the world. The professors of Oxford, Cambridge, Harvard and Yale Universities did not pack their bags and come racing to the hospital to peer over the side of my cradle. Once I got home, at no stage did the then US President Ronald Reagan knock on the door and ask my parents if he could give me some presents.

Of course they didn't. It would have been ridiculous for them to do so. The powerful and learned people of AD 1981 would have been crazy to have dropped everything, cleared their diaries, and come to see me so that they could get on their knees and worship me.

WISE OR CRAZY?

But that's exactly what these "wise men" did in around 0 AD. We don't know much about them: we don't know where they came from except that it was in "the east";

we don't know what they were called; we don't actually know how many of them there were. We don't even quite know what they did—the word "Magi" suggests they were astrologers or professors or priests, or a mixture of all three.

But what we do know is that these men travelled hundreds of miles, possibly for months and months, with expensive gifts, to see… a baby born in a small town in an insignificant country in a far corner of the Roman Empire.

What we do know is that when they got to the house where Mary was staying with Jesus (it seems he'd been upgraded from a manger to a proper cradle), these wealthy and knowledgeable men got down on their knees and worshipped this child. "We have come to worship him", they had told King Herod—and that's exactly what they did.

That's ridiculous. Stupid. Crazy.

Well, it would have been, if it hadn't been for the fact that, as we've seen, this child was different. This child had been born "king of the Jews"—the Messiah himself. And, though these wise men weren't Jews, they knew this child mattered for them too.

If Jesus is the Messiah, then what these Magi did wasn't ridiculous or stupid or crazy. It was really very sensible. If Jesus is the Messiah, the right response is to worship him.

And that goes for us, too.

We, like the wise men, probably aren't from Israel. We may not know very much about what God's prophets said (though we can find their words in the Old Testament). We may tend to look to the stars and guess at what's going on, instead of reading what God says in his Bible.

But if Jesus is the Messiah, the right response is to copy the Magi—and worship him.

WHAT IS WORSHIP?

But what does "worship" mean? For years, I thought it meant going to church, being fairly dull, and possibly wearing sandals. But the Magi show us it's something quite different.

It means giving up our time for Jesus, just as they did.

It means putting ourselves out for Jesus, asking for more knowledge about Jesus, and giving Jesus the best we have to offer—just as they did.

It means letting Jesus shape how we use our days, our minds, our wallets.

In other words, it means putting Jesus at the centre of our lives—enjoying him as the best thing we have in life.

And, crucially, it means accepting that Jesus is our King, our ruler—just as they did.

THE WISE OPTION

Lots of people think you have to be a bit dim to worship Jesus.

But these "wise men" would probably say that if God did come into our world as the person Jesus, it's wiser to worship him than ignore him. And that if we can't understand everything about Jesus, maybe it's not because we're clever and it's all silly but because he's God and we're not.

Perhaps the wise thing to do is to look at the evidence and think things through, instead of dismissing the whole thing. Perhaps the wise thing to do is to accept that we may well never understand *everything* but that we can understand *enough* to see and know and experience for ourselves that Jesus is the person who makes sense of our lives.

If Jesus is the Messiah, perhaps the wise thing to do is to worship him with all we have, just as those Magi did.

It's what wise people have been doing ever since—no matter how rich and powerful they may be. As Queen Elizabeth II—the longest-serving British monarch in history and the most famous woman in the world in her lifetime—put it, "For me the teachings of Christ and my own personal accountability before God provide a framework in which I try to lead my life." In other words, *I may be Queen, but what Jesus says guides my life more than my own feelings, preferences or thoughts.* Or as her great-great-grandmother Victoria is reported to have said, she was looking forward to meeting Jesus "so that I can cast my crown before him". Elizabeth and Victoria both recognised that even as queens, they had a ruler: someone who deserved their everything—even their crowns.

But not all rulers react to Jesus being the Messiah that way. And, as the Magi bowed down to Jesus in Bethlehem, back in Jerusalem one king was planning to do something very different to him...

SCENE FIVE

A DARKER CHRISTMAS

King Herod

The year after I played a donkey's rear end, I hit the big time. I was chosen to be King Herod. I had to shout and scowl and stamp my feet—a role that required me to make use of the full range of my acting abilities.

But my lines missed out a huge chunk of what happened in history. There's a part that never appears in children's nativity plays. Even lots of churches skip over it with their adults each December. After all, massacres don't exactly get people into the festive spirit.

This is where Christmas history gets darker...

WHAT REALLY HAPPENED

After the Magi had met Jesus, **they returned to their country by another route,** because they had **been** warned in a dream not to go back to Herod.

They weren't the only people leaving Bethlehem. **When they had gone, an angel of the Lord appeared to Joseph in a dream.**

"Get up," he said, **"take the child and his mother and escape to Egypt. Stay there until I tell you, for Herod is going to search for the child to kill him."**

Joseph did as he was told. **He got up, took the child and his mother during the night and left for Egypt.**

When Herod realised that he had been outwitted by the Magi, he was furious, and he gave orders to kill all the boys in Bethlehem and its vicinity who were two years old and under, in accordance with the time he had learned from the Magi.

Herod's orders were carried out to the letter. All through Bethlehem you could hear **weeping and great mourning** of mothers **refusing to be comforted**. It was a massacre.

But Herod failed to achieve his aim. God's Son Jesus was in Egypt, where he **stayed until the death of Herod. After Herod died, an angel of the Lord appeared in a dream to Joseph in Egypt and said, "Get up, take the child and his mother and go to the land of Israel, for those who were trying to take the child's life are dead."**

So he got up, and went to the land of Israel. He went and lived in Nazareth. Finally, Joseph, Mary and Jesus were home.

Read the full story: Matthew 2 v 12-23

WHY IT REALLY MATTERS

MASS GRAVE

It's a horrific, shocking twist—the cold-blooded murder of what would have been dozens of children.

There must have been a grave near Bethlehem filled with the small bodies of these little ones. We see such graves from time to time on television; I once even visited a mass grave in which some of my relatives are buried. It's a tragic fact that a massacre like this is not an infrequent event through human history.

And the question is: why? Why did Herod dislike Jesus so much that he wanted to kill him? Why was Herod prepared to kill any number of boys just to be sure he'd taken out one particular toddler?

TURF WAR

The answer to that question is one we might not like because it involves us. The answer is that what we're watching in this episode of the Christmas story is a turf war.

Herod was king of Israel; it was his country. He ruled it. Yes, he ruled it under the Romans, but most of the time he could ignore that fact. Israel was his.

But now the Messiah had been born. God's true King of the Jews had arrived. And ultimately, Israel belonged to him (as did the whole world). Jesus had the greatest claim to be the ruler of Israel. Not the Romans. Not Herod.

So Herod had a decision to make.

He could, like Queen Elizabeth did 2,000 years later, accept that Jesus was the king over him. He could carry on being king but under Jesus' authority, taking the decisions Jesus wanted him to, allowing his life to be shaped by Jesus. He could give his turf, his Israel, to Jesus, worshipping him as Messiah.

Or Herod could resist Jesus. He could fight Jesus. He could push Jesus out of Israel so that he could carry on being the only ruler.

He chose the second option. He tried to get rid of Jesus; that's why Bethlehem's toddlers were massacred. Herod's brutal orders were motivated by his refusal to let Jesus be his ruler.

That attitude is what the Bible calls "sin". It's the attitude which resists Jesus' rule, which would rather Jesus didn't exist, and which refuses to accept that Jesus, God's Messiah, is the rightful ruler.

It's the attitude which says, "This is my turf, Jesus, not yours. I will not let you have it. I will fight you."

HEROD AND ME

Herod had a lot of turf—the whole of Israel. I don't have much at all—but I do have my own life. In my life, I do and say and treat people how I choose. I'm the ruler. It's mine.

Except that if Jesus is the Messiah—if he's God's

Son, who created me and created the world I live in—
then actually my life belongs to him. He has the right
to say how I should live and what I should do and how
I should treat others in his world. He has a greater
claim over my life than anyone else—a greater claim
even than mine.

So when it comes to the turf of my own life, I have
a choice. I can accept Jesus' rule, worshipping him as
my king—like the Magi. Or I can resist and refuse his
rule—like Herod.

Naturally, I choose the second option.

I rule my own life. I sin. Because I was brought up to
have manners, I do it quite politely: I'm not rude about
Jesus, I'm often quite nice to other people, and I work
hard. Sometimes, when what Jesus says happens to
agree with what I already think, I do what he'd like. But
at the end of the day, I want me to be in charge of life,
not Jesus.

So I act as if he isn't the King. I act as if he's dead.

HEROD AND US

And the hard truth is that this is what we all do,
naturally. When it comes to the turf of our own lives,
we are all mini-Herods.

That doesn't lead us to ruin people's lives through
committing mass murder. But our refusal to let Jesus
be our ruler does lead us to ruin other people's lives in
smaller, less noticeable ways. There's the person whose
heart we selfishly broke, who can't quite put it behind

them. The person we laughed at, shattering their confidence. The person we trod on to get a promotion at work, who's now twisted by bitterness. The person we simply never noticed and unconsciously ignored, who feels lonely and worthless. There are countless little things we do each day which make the lives of those around us a bit less satisfying than God designed them to be.

I wish this didn't describe me. I wish I could look at my life and truthfully say I've never acted in those ways. But when I'm honest, I know that I can't. I'm guessing you can't either.

And all these outward actions (and many others) are signs of an inward attitude—an attitude that looks at our life and looks at Jesus Christ and says, "This is my turf, Jesus, not yours. I will not let you have it."

It's a hard truth to accept; but it explains what we see in the world around us, and it explains what we sometimes notice in our own hearts. We're sinful, just like Herod.

And, just like Herod, we're fighting a turf war that we can't win.

A LOSING BATTLE

Herod must have thought he had all the power: he had priests to advise him, wise men to inform him and soldiers to kill for him. But he couldn't do what he wanted; he couldn't kill Jesus off. Because compared to God, he had no power at all. God was in control—

sending angels, speaking through dreams, moving his Son to safety.

King Herod tried hard to get rid of God's King; but he couldn't. And by the time Joseph brought his family back to Nazareth, only one of those two kings was still alive—and it wasn't Herod. The turf that Herod had killed to keep was taken away from him.

I wonder what God said to Herod after he'd died. I wonder if Herod tried to find a way to excuse how he'd treated God's Son, and how he'd treated others as he fought God's Son. I doubt there was anything he could have said.

And, like Herod, we can spend a whole lifetime resisting Jesus' right to rule us. But, however powerful we are, we can't resist Jesus for ever. Just as it did for Herod, the time will come when each of us dies.

I wonder what you're planning to say to God when *you* meet him. Is there any possible excuse you and I will be able to offer for how we've treated God's Son, and how we've treated others as we've fought him?

It won't help to argue that our actions have been less serious than those of others. Or that we did some good things among the bad. Or that we had thought about Jesus from time to time—or even that we believed he was quite special.

Our sinfulness means that none of us will deserve a place in the kingdom of the Christ we've rejected. There'll be no eternity enjoying all his goodness and gifts—of which the best of this life is just a tiny glimmer. Instead, there'll be an eternity outside his kingdom, enduring an existence with nothing good in it at all—of which the worst of this life is just a shadow.

This is a hard truth—it makes death something to be terrified of. It's an unpopular truth—but that doesn't stop it being true. I need rescuing from the conse-quences of my rejection of Jesus, the Messiah. We all do. So it's great to remember what the angel said to those shepherds: "Today in the town of David a *Saviour* has been born".

Jesus was born not only to rule us but to rescue us. And it would be the end of his life, not the beginning, which would show what the angel had meant.

A STRANGE PREDICTION

The Old Man

There's only one old man who gets a mention at Christmas. He wears red... brings the presents... and, bizarrely, often pops up at random points in nativity plays. Santa Claus may not be real (sorry if that's news to you), but he's pretty popular.

Of course, Santa was nowhere to be seen at the first Christmas. But there was an old man at the heart of the real events. Not Santa, but Simeon. And Simeon didn't do presents.

But he did do predictions...

WHAT REALLY HAPPENED

Back before they fled to Egypt, Mary and Joseph, as tradition demanded, brought Jesus to the temple in

Jerusalem **to present him to the Lord and to offer a sacrifice** in recognition that their baby was, as all babies are, a gift from God to them.

There was a man in Jerusalem called Simeon. It had been revealed to him by the Holy Spirit that he would not die before he had seen the Lord's Messiah.

That day, **he went into the temple courts. When the parents brought in the child Jesus, Simeon took him in his arms and praised God, saying:**

"Sovereign Lord, as you have promised, you may now dismiss your servant in peace. For my eyes have seen your salvation."

Then Simeon **said to Mary, his mother: "This child is destined to be spoken against, so that the thoughts of many hearts will be revealed.**

"And a sword will pierce your own soul too."

It was a strange, unsettling prediction.

And three decades later, Mary discovered just what he had meant. A few hundred yards from where Simeon had held Jesus in his arms, Mary watched as soldiers executed her son. She'd sat next to Jesus' manger; now, thirty years later, she was standing next to his cross.

When Jesus saw his mother there, and one of his closest friends, John, **standing near by, he said to her, "Woman, here is your son,"** and to John, **"Here is your mother."**

From that time on, John **took her into his home** to care for her as part of his family.

From all around the cross, the mocking and insults rained down on the dying man. The religious leaders had hated Jesus ever since he had started explaining that he was the Messiah. So they'd spread lies to have him found guilty, and were enjoying getting rid of him:

"He saved others; let him save himself if he is God's Messiah, the Chosen One."

He didn't save himself; he stayed nailed to the wooden cross. But as Jesus hung there—mocked, naked and bleeding—something strange happened above him.

It was now about noon, and darkness came over the whole land, for the sun stopped shining. This wasn't some kind of natural eclipse—the timing was wrong for that. It was strange... and it was significant. As the Jews who were watching knew, God had already explained it. Centuries before he had warned them—the people he'd rescued, looked after and spoken to—that he wouldn't go on putting up with their sin, with their determination not to live with him as God.

He warned them that a day was coming when he'd pour out his anger at the way people had treated each other, his world, and him. Since they'd rejected living with God as their King, he'd reject them from being in his eternal kingdom. He'd take away all the good things they had enjoyed from him without ever thinking of or thanking him.

God had promised that **"in that day, I will make the sun go down at noon and darken the earth in broad daylight"**.

Now God's right anger, his punishment, had come.

And yet, apart from the darkness, everything seemed normal. Was that it? Perhaps it was a false alarm!

The darkness lasted for three hours.

Then, **with a loud cry, Jesus breathed his last. One of the soldiers pierced Jesus' side with a spear, bringing a sudden flow of blood and water.**

God's Messiah, the man Jesus, Mary's son, was dead. And, her soul pierced, she stood there, **watching these things**.

Read the full story: Luke 2 v 21-40, 23 v 35, 44-49; John 19 v 25-37; Mark 15 v 25-41; Amos 8 v 9-14

WHY IT REALLY MATTERS

THE PIERCING SWORD

One of the worst things in the world is to lose a child. Someone once wrote that it's like losing a leg: you get used to it, but the loss and the pain never really go.

Mary knew what it was like to have her son die—more than that, she knew what it was like to have to watch it. She knew an unimaginable grief—what that old man Simeon had described thirty years earlier, while holding her baby, as having a sword pierce her soul.

She must have felt that emotional sword as Jesus—

who'd lived a blameless life but was killed because the Jewish leaders didn't want him to be their Messiah—had real six-inch nails hammered through his wrists and his ankles.

She must have felt that emotional sword as Jesus had a real spear pushed through his side.

And she must have felt that emotional sword as Jesus hung on the cross as the sky went black—as her son experienced a spiritual torment far worse than either his physical pain or his mother's emotional pain.

THE ANGER OF GOD

The sky going black as the Jewish leaders killed God's Messiah should be of no surprise. The darkness signalled that God's anger had come. Of course God the Father was angry! His own Son, who he loved, was being unfairly executed. Wouldn't you be angry?

The surprise is not that God the Father was angry; the surprise is *who* God was angry with. His anger and his punishment didn't fall on the people who'd fought a turf war against his Messiah. They didn't die. No, God the Father's anger and punishment fell on the man who *was* his Messiah. His anger fell on his Son—on the only person of his day, of any day, who had never done anything wrong. The shock is that *Jesus* died.

On the cross, God the Son chose to bear the punishment that people deserve for their sin—for their refusal to let him rule. Jesus experienced the hell of being shut out of his Father's kindness and kingdom.

He traded places. He was punished instead of sinful people.

God's Son took God's anger so that we don't have to.

WHAT THE CROSS SHOWS

Stand next to Mary for a moment and watch the Messiah dying under God's punishment. His agony on the cross shows us how horrific life without God will be. It shows us what you and I face beyond death for trying to push him off our turf: a future outside God's kingdom.

But his cross also shows us that this doesn't need to be our future. When we die, instead of standing before God with nothing to say and no excuses to make, we can stand there and say:

> *"The Messiah I resisted took hell instead of me. The Messiah I resisted saved me from hell. The Messiah I resisted has given me a place in his perfect kingdom."*

When the angel told those shepherds that "a Saviour has been born to you ... he is the Messiah, the Lord", he was pointing towards the cross. The baby lying in a manger at the first Christmas had come to hang on the cross on the first Good Friday. Jesus came not only to rule people but to rescue them. Not only to tell people about his eternal perfect kingdom, but to make a way for sinful people like us to get into that kingdom.

He came to be the Saviour. He chose to die so that our death does not need to be a terrifying dead-end—the end of all hope and joy and peace. It can be the doorway to perfect life in Christ's kingdom.

GOD'S SCRIPT

It's ironic when you think about it. God the Father was in control at Jesus' birth, so Herod's attempts to kill him failed. And God the Father was still in control at Jesus' death, which is the only reason why the religious leaders' attempts to kill him succeeded. The script had been written not in a palace or a temple but in heaven.

God the Most High was in control of every detail. And he was in control three days later when some women who had been friends with Jesus went to the tomb he was buried in. They went to rub spices into his body to stop it starting to smell in the heat.

But they didn't find a corpse.

Instead, just as Mary had seen all those years ago at home in Nazareth as a teenager, they saw an angel.

And the angel said to the women, **"You are looking for Jesus, who was crucified. He is not here; he has risen, just as he said. Come and see the place where he lay."**

So the women hurried away from the tomb, afraid yet filled with joy, and ran to tell his disciples. Suddenly Jesus met them.

"Greetings," he said.

They came to him, clasped his feet and (just as the Magi had thirty years before) **worshipped him.***

* Read the full story: Matthew 28 v 1-20

Mary knew what it was to watch her son die. But amazingly, she also knew what it was to have a son rise from the dead. God's plan had always been for his Son to be born as the Messiah, the Ruler; to die to be people's Saviour, the Rescuer; and to rise to eternal life beyond death so that he can welcome people who worship him into perfect life in his kingdom.

THE BABY GREW UP

Jesus

It was a big event for the school. A nativity performed in a hall a few miles away, with local VIPs and the press attending. It was hard work helping the children learn their lines, making costumes and navigating the parental politics around who would be chosen to play Mary. But now all was ready, the guests were gathered, and the nativity could begin.

It was only now that the organisers realised something was missing. They had left the doll they were using for Jesus back at school. Miles away. And there was no time to go back and get it.

Fortunately, in nativity plays you don't really need Jesus. He has no lines. The focus is on the other characters—Mary and Joseph, the angels, shepherds, Magi. Afterwards, the teachers weren't sure whether anyone had even noticed that there'd been no Jesus in the manger that year.

WHAT REALLY HAPPENED

When he was around thirty, **Jesus went into Galilee**, the area around Nazareth, **proclaiming the good news of God.**

"**The time has come,**" he said. "**The kingdom of God has come near. Repent and believe the good news!**"

Read the full story: Mark 1 v 1-20

WHY IT REALLY MATTERS

There are four historical biographies, or Gospels, of Jesus in the Bible. One of them was written by a very early follower of Jesus, a man named Mark. And the startling thing about his Gospel is that he completely ignores the Christmas story!

Mark misses out the angels, the shepherds, the Magi. There's no mention of Jesus' parents, his birth, or his childhood.

Perhaps Mark wants us to remember that the baby grew up. Perhaps he wants to put the man Jesus centre stage, for us to hear what he said and what he did. Perhaps he doesn't want to leave us the option of pretending Jesus stayed a baby, who never said or did anything.

Mark takes us straight to Jesus the man. And the first

words he records Jesus saying sum up why Jesus was born, and why he died, and why it really matters for each one of us:

> *"The time has come. The kingdom of God has come near. Repent and believe the good news!"*

"THE TIME HAS COME"

With the arrival of Jesus, God broke into history as a human. There's no need to guess who God is. The time has come for us to know. There's no need to wonder if God will ever sort out this world. The time has come for him to do it.

"THE KINGDOM OF GOD HAS COME NEAR"

With the arrival of Jesus, the perfect kingdom of God began to be built. In what he did—healing people, welcoming people, loving people—Jesus gave a glimpse of how amazing life in his kingdom is. In how he died— taking the punishment of God that we deserve, experiencing the hell that we should experience—Jesus gave us a way to be part of his kingdom for ever.

And life in God's kingdom is the kind of life that deep down we're each looking for. Perfect, fulfilling, satisfying life—the life that we're all, one way or another, striving to find—was offered to us at the first Christmas.

The time has come to know God. The perfect kingdom of God has been opened up for anyone to enjoy—including you. But how do we get into it? Two things are needed...

"REPENT"

To "repent" is to change your mind completely—for your way of thinking to turn around. If you want to be part of his kingdom, now and beyond death, Jesus says you need to repent—to turn away from living with yourself as ruler and towards living with him as your King.

Repenting means giving your life to Jesus and worshipping him: looking to him when you make decisions, leaving it to him to tell you how to act, and treating him as the most valuable aspect of, or person in, your life.

Repenting is a great thing to do. It means the ruler of your life will no longer be someone who doesn't actually know that much about life and who knows nothing about the future (i.e. you!). Instead, the one in charge of you will be someone who knows everything about life and who controls the future—Jesus the Messiah, the Son of God.

But repenting is a hard thing to do. It means that you won't simply do what you want, or what's easiest, or what's most popular any more. You won't be in charge of your diary, your wallet or your heart. It means there'll be times when you want to disagree with what Jesus says, but you obey him anyway. And there'll be times when you seem to be missing out.

If you know someone who's repented—who lives as a Christian—you'll know that they make some decisions that can seem quite strange. They often don't do things that most people say make you feel good in life. And yet you might also have noticed that they seem more satisfied and more secure than people who are chasing wealth, affirmation, sexual fulfilment or power. Repentance makes a real difference.

"BELIEVE THE GOOD NEWS"

Everybody trusts in things. If you're sitting down to read this, you're currently trusting in your chair or sofa for your comfort—you believe it will bear your weight. If you're married, you're trusting in your husband or wife for your heart—you believe them when they say they love you and are faithful to you. If you work for a living, you're trusting your employer for your income—you believe them when they say you'll get paid.

What are you trusting in for your death? What or who are you banking on to make the prospect of your death ok? Maybe it's yourself—you believe that being a pretty nice person will mean it's all ok. Maybe it's an idea— you believe there's nothing the other side of death, so you don't need to worry.

Christians believe in good news about a person: someone who knows what's on the other side of death because he's been there—someone who knows how to get through death because he's done it.

The good news of the Bible is that Jesus has done everything necessary to give you perfect life in God's eternal kingdom. You don't need to try to gain it yourself. You don't need to be good enough. You don't need to go to church a certain number of times. You don't need to keep lots of religious rules.

You just need to "believe the good news": to trust that Jesus the Messiah has done it all for you—that when he died, he died in your place, taking the punishment from God that you deserve, and that when he rose, he rose to give you life in his kingdom.

HOW ABOUT YOU?

So, when Jesus calls people to repent and believe, he's calling them to accept him as their ruler—the one who's in charge of their life—and their rescuer—the one who will bring them through death.

In some ways, it'd be easier for us if Jesus had never said anything—if he'd stayed in his manger, kept quiet and never grown up. But he did grow up, and he does speak. He tells us that in him we can see God and see God's kingdom. He challenges me, and you, to repent and believe.

I can still remember the evening years ago when someone asked me, "What are you going to do about Jesus?" By that point, I'd understood for a while what really happened: that Jesus had really existed and had lived and died and risen in history. And slowly, I'd come to see that these were not just historical details, like the year the Spanish Armada sailed towards England or the date Julius Caesar was assassinated. Jesus' life was more than a piece of quiz trivia. It mattered.

But I hadn't done anything about it. It had made no difference to my life or to my future—until that friend of mine said, "What are you going to do about Jesus?"

It was a blunt question! But I suddenly realised that it had an obvious answer. I needed to repent and believe: to accept Jesus as *my* ruler and *my* rescuer. It was no good just knowing *about* him; I needed to actually know *him*, to start following and trusting in and speaking to and listening to him.

It was the most important decision I ever made. In many ways, it was a decision that made my life more difficult. But in every way, it has made my life more fulfilling, satisfying and exciting. Looking back, it was easily the best decision I've ever made.

So, I'll finish this last chapter with that same blunt question: what are you going to do about Jesus?

Maybe you need to think things through a bit more— to check out some of the facts and ask more questions. Over the page, there are a few ways you could do that.

But maybe you know that the time has come for you to make the decision—to repent and believe. You know the time has come to tell Jesus that you want him to be your ruler and your rescuer. In other words, to become a Christian.

Why not speak to him now?

WHAT NEXT?

Thanks for reading this book. I hope that you've enjoyed it and that it's informed and even excited you about Jesus.

I'm guessing you fall into one of two categories...

1. Maybe you're someone who would like to keep looking into Christianity before making your mind up about what you believe. Here are a few ways you can keep thinking things through...

Read a Gospel. There are four historical biographies of Jesus' life—Matthew, Mark, Luke and John (this book has used parts of all of them). Why not grab one and read through it? The shortest one is Mark, which takes around two hours to read. Or you could listen to an audio version.

Pray. That may seem strange! But why not speak to God and ask him, if he is there, to help you to see the truth about who he is, who Jesus is, and what life is all about?

Head to a church. Find a church that takes the Bible seriously as God's word, that talks a lot about Jesus, and where you feel welcomed (even if you don't agree with everything you hear). That's a great place to ask questions and to see the difference that Jesus makes to real people's real lives.

Join a Hope Explored course. This is an informal, relaxed, three-session introduction to Christianity, where you can ask questions, discuss, or simply listen. If you want a more in-depth walk through a Gospel, join Christianity Explored. You can find a course near you on the website www.christianityexplored.org (which also features some video answers to questions lots of people ask, and some real-life stories of people who became Christians in various ways, at various stages, for various reasons).

Look at the historical evidence. If you'd like to look in more detail at how we know that the Gospels are real history, a great book to read is *Is Christmas Unbeliev-able?* by Rebecca McLaughlin. You can get a copy at: www.thegoodbook.co.uk/is-christmas-unbelievable.

2. Maybe, though, you're reading this page as someone who has repented and believed—you've become a Christian. That's fantastic! It can all seem a bit strange at first (or at least, it did for me). The best advice I can give you is to find a church near you that bases all it says on the Bible (in the same way this book does). The

people there will help you to keep getting to know Jesus, your ruler and rescuer, and encourage you to see how you can worship him. If you'd like a hand with finding a church like this, just email hello@thegoodbook.co.uk.

YES, BUT...

Isn't a lot of this made up?

When you read something, it helps to know what you're reading. I wouldn't use a car manual to tell me how to cook a roast dinner; I wouldn't use a recipe book to help me change the oil in my car!

Throughout this book, you'll have seen me talking about what the four Gospels in the Bible tell us about what really happened at the first Christmas. And I talk about what they say as though those things really happened—as though they were history. Why?

Because that's the type of books the Gospels are. Here's how one of them, written by a man called Luke, begins:

Many have undertaken to draw up an account of the things that have been fulfilled among us, just as they were handed down to us by those who from the first were eye witnesses and servants of the word. With this in mind, since I myself have carefully investigated everything from the beginning, I too

decided to write an orderly account for you, most
excellent Theophilus, so that you may know the
certainty of the things you have been taught.

(Luke 1 v 1-4)

Luke was writing his Gospel about Jesus for someone he knew—a guy called Theophilus. And what he wanted to do was to let Theophilus know what had actually happened to Jesus. He'd researched it all, and he'd spoken to eye witnesses who'd seen what really happened; now he'd written it all out in an "orderly" way.

He was writing a historical biography of Jesus' life. That's his claim.

Now of course, Luke could have just made it all up, just as I could rewrite history to make my dad a Premier League star instead of a retired computing teacher. But it's completely unlikely that Luke would have done that, for two reasons.

First, at the time Luke (and the other Gospel writers) were writing their historical biographies of Jesus, you could very easily get killed for being a Christian. Why make up something that could land you in prison, facing torture and death?! It would be like me making up a back-story for my dad which claimed that he was a high-level al-Qaeda terrorist, and that I was working for him.

Second, Luke was a Christian. It's easy to think that this would make it more likely that he'd made his Gospel up. Actually, it makes it less likely. If Luke thought this guy Jesus was God, he'd really, really care about getting the facts about him correct. He wouldn't want to make mistakes about someone so important. He'd be more careful to tell historical facts, not less.

One final thing that can make us even more confident that Luke and the others are telling us historical facts is that their stories fit with other historical accounts of the time. The events they talk about fit with other histories. The people they talk about, like Roman emperors and Jewish priests, are real people. Jesus himself is mentioned by both Roman and Jewish historians who would probably rather he hadn't lived; so he himself definitely existed. And the details of the places the Gospel-writers wrote about, like how there were two towns next to each other with the same name, check out with archaeological research.

So, the Gospels claim to be historical fact; they sound like historical fact; and they check out with other histories as historical fact—which is why, in this book, I treat what they say about Jesus as historical fact. Strange facts, amazing facts, challenging facts, but still facts!

If you'd like to think in more detail about why we can be confident that the Gospels are history, here are a couple of great books to read:

Can We Trust What the Gospels Say about Jesus? (you can get a copy at www.thegoodbook.co.uk/trust-jesus-gospels)

The Case for Christ (www.thegoodbook.co.uk/case-for-christ)

YES, BUT...

Surely Jesus didn't actually
come back from the dead?!

One of Jesus' earliest followers, Paul, wrote that "if Christ has not been raised ... faith is futile" (1 Corinthians 15 v 17).

The resurrection of Jesus back to life is the point where the whole of Christianity stands or falls. And the resurrection of Jesus is the point where lots of people say, "That's just ridiculous. The rest of the story, ok— but not a dead man coming back to life!"

No one can prove beyond any doubt that Jesus rose from the dead. But that's because no one can prove anything beyond any doubt. I can't prove my wife loves me—but, based on the evidence, I believe that she does. You can't prove that you're not a butterfly who's dreaming it's a human—but, based on the evidence, you believe that you're not (hopefully!).

So in thinking about whether Jesus rose or not, it's

about what we think is the *most likely* explanation for what happened on that day in history.

And people have come up with some pretty good explanations. Below are the best I've found. For each, I've laid out the explanation as well as I can, and then mentioned the questions that they don't really answer.

1. THERE WAS NO EMPTY TOMB: THE WOMEN WENT TO THE WRONG ONE

The women were tired and upset when they saw where Jesus was laid. When they went to visit the body a couple of days later, they went to the wrong tomb. The body wasn't there; they put two and two together and made 648, and told everyone he'd been raised.

Unanswered questions:

- *They weren't expecting him to rise. If you had gone to the wrong tomb, wouldn't you just find the right one, not announce a resurrection?!*

- *When Jesus' followers announced a month or so later that Jesus had risen, why didn't the authorities simply go to the tomb they'd put soldiers outside, get the body and disprove the resurrection?*

2. THE TOMB WAS EMPTY BECAUSE JESUS WASN'T REALLY DEAD

Jesus didn't die on the cross—he just fainted and then came round in the cool tomb. He then spent time with his friends and ate and walked with them, and then went away and lived somewhere else. His friends assumed he'd gone to heaven and started talking about the resurrection.

Unanswered questions:

- *The Romans were good at crucifying people. Did they really think Jesus was dead when he wasn't?*

- *One of the soldiers near the cross stuck a spear into his side. Could a man who'd been stabbed in the heart survive without medical help for three days and then walk out?*

- *Could a man who'd been nailed to a cross go for a long walk with friends two days later?*

- *Why didn't the guards at the tomb notice Jesus limping out?*

3. THE TOMB WAS EMPTY BECAUSE THE BODY WAS TAKEN BY THE AUTHORITIES

The leaders knew Jesus had predicted his resurrection. So they moved the body to make sure there could be no scam by his followers. That left an empty tomb; and the disciples took advantage of this, or misunderstood this, and went around saying Jesus had risen.

Unanswered question:

- *If the authorities had the body, why didn't they produce it when people started believing Jesus had risen? That would have stopped the rumours of a resurrection!*

4. THE TOMB WAS EMPTY BECAUSE THE BODY WAS TAKEN BY GRAVE-ROBBERS

Bodies weren't valuable, but grave-clothes were. So some grave-robbers stole the body. The tomb was left empty for the women to find, and a legend was born.

Unanswered question:

- *Why, when the empty tomb was discovered, were the valuable grave-clothes still there? Why hadn't the grave-robbers taken the only thing of value in the tomb?*

5. THE TOMB WAS EMPTY BECAUSE THE BODY WAS TAKEN BY THE DISCIPLES

Jesus' followers had much to gain from a "resurrection". So they stole the body, announced the resurrection and said Jesus had appeared to them several times, and that he'd now gone away again, back to heaven. And the resurrection lie enabled them to set up a new religion—Christianity.

Unanswered questions:

- *Could the disciples, who were terrified and had run away, really have managed to pull off stealing a body from under the noses of some Roman guards?*

- *If the disciples had made up the Gospels of Jesus in the Bible, why do they come across in them as scared, disloyal and weak? Wouldn't you make up something more impressive about yourself?*

- *If the disciples had made this up, they knew for a fact Jesus hadn't risen. Yet almost all of them ended up being killed for saying he'd come back to life and was God. Wouldn't at least one of them have admitted it was all made up to avoid being crucified, stoned or beheaded?*

6. THE DISCIPLES DIDN'T REALLY SEE JESUS: IT WAS A HALLUCINATION

The "appearances" of Jesus were simple hallucinations. After all, the disciples were emotional, tired and grieving—and they saw what they wanted to see.

Unanswered questions:

- *Medically, people simply don't hallucinate the same thing at the same time. Did dozens (and on one occasion hundreds) of adults really have an identical hallucination at exactly the same time?*

- *Why was the tomb empty? If this was a hallucination, the body would still have been in the tomb.*

7. THE TOMB WAS EMPTY BECAUSE JESUS HAD RISEN BACK TO LIFE

This is what Jesus' friends claimed had happened, even when they faced gruesome deaths for saying it. It explains the empty tomb; and it explains the appearances of Jesus after his death.

Unanswered question:

- *Do people really rise from the dead? It's not exactly a normal event!*

(To which my answer, for what it's worth, is that if you were God, you could raise someone from the dead without difficulty. And if you wanted to prove you were God, you'd need to do something amazing and abnormal—like promising to die and rise again, and then actually doing that.)

thegoodbook
COMPANY

Thanks for reading this book. We hope you enjoyed it, and found it helpful.

Most people want to find answers to the big questions of life: Who are we? Why are we here? How should we live? But for many valid reasons we are often unable to find the time or the right space to think positively and carefully about them.

Perhaps you have questions that you need an answer for. Perhaps you have met Christians who have seemed unsympathetic or incomprehensible. Or maybe you are someone who has grown up believing, but need help to make things a little clearer.

At The Good Book Company, we're passionate about producing materials that help people of all ages and stages understand the heart of the Christian message, which is found in the pages of the Bible.

Whoever you are, and wherever you are at when it comes to these big questions, we hope we can help. As a publisher we want to help you look at the good book that is the Bible because we're convinced that as we meet the person who stands at its heart—Jesus Christ—we find the clearest answers to our biggest questions.

Visit our website to discover the range of books, videos and other resources we produce, or visit our partner site www.christianityexplored.org for a clear explanation of who Jesus is and why he came.

Thanks again for reading,

Your friends at The Good Book Company

thegoodbook.com | thegoodbook.co.uk
thegoodbook.com.au | thegoodbook.co.nz | thegoodbook.co.in

WWW.CHRISTIANITYEXPLORED.ORG

Our partner site is a great place to explore the Christian faith, with powerful testimonies and answers to difficult questions.